A Word to the

How to Bring Your Husband Down from the Rooftop

PASTOR BERNARD BLACKMON

FIRST EDITION

ISBN: 978-0-9981815-8-5

Library of Congress Control Number: 2016963689

Published by

P.O. Box 2839, Apopka, FL 32704

Printed in the United States of America

Disclaimer: The views and opinions expressed in this book are solely those of the author and other contributors. These views and opinions do not necessarily represent those of Certa Publishing. Please note that Certa Publishing's publishing style capitalizes certain pronouns in Scripture that refer to the Father, Son, and Holy Spirit, and may differ from some publishers' styles.

Table of Contents

Dedication

A Word to the Wife is dedicated to my covenant partner and lovely wife Vicky. The 20 years spent with you have proven to be an amazing experience of undeniable love with you being by my side through many tests, trials, and triumphant victories. I thank you for your support and unconditional love with every endeavor God allows me to pursue.

This book is dedicated to women in different phases of their lives, who are seeking understanding on how an effective bond with their spouses can bring forth a rewarding marriage. My prayer is you will gain wisdom that will be beneficial to sustaining a successful relationship in your marriage.

Epigraph

Proverbs 21:9

"It is better to dwell in a corner of the housetop, than with a brawling woman in a wide house."

Preface

What you hold in your hand would take way before the year 1996, up until now, for this insight to be birthed and made available to you. This is actually the byproduct from being a newly disciple convert, who was trying to grow spiritually in the faith after extensive studies in Proverbs. At the time, I was mentored by my cousin Doug when I first became a Christian. He shared with me that the Book of Proverbs contained chapters just like the calendar has 31 days. He encouraged me to choose one of the months that had 31 days and start reading. It sounded easy enough.

So upon his suggestion, I chose a month that in fact had 31 days and began reading a chapter a day. Of course, this was all taking place before I would marry my beautiful bride. As I began taking a closer look at the text in the scripture, my attention was repeatedly drawn over and over again to a husband being on the "rooftop." After reflecting on this for several years and asking why the Bible would say in Proverbs 21:9, *It is better to dwell in a corner of the housetop, than with a brawling woman in a wide house,* in addition to highlighting and rereading the scripture, the subject of this book was placed on my heart.

The more I thought about a "rooftop husband," the more I saw it happening all around me. At times, I actually saw myself as being the rooftop husband. So about 6 years ago, I was graced with the understanding of what a wife needs to do to handle a husband that is on the "rooftop." I have the answer of the hidden truth that I have come to know of what many wives need in order to bring the fire they long for in their marriage.

I am trusting these words will be the key that unlocks many unanswered prayers. This was carefully written with you in mind and handled with love and care. I still read Proverbs today and it was through that practice that allows you to read *A Word to the Wife*. – Pastor B

Acknowledgement

I am so grateful to God and honor Him for allowing me the opportunity to utilize the words He has given me to share with you. I want to show appreciation to my wife Vicky for giving me the release to share my heart and thoughts with you. I am so thankful this book is not just a mere reflection of us, but a revelation to marriages everywhere for hope and healing that will impact people's lives.

While I certainly, am not able to even begin to name all the wonderful people that played an integral role for the birthing of this book, I certainly appreciate who you are and what you have been to me as it relates to the feedback you provided as I shared the concept of this book with you. I want to recognize Larry, Christina, and Miji for your contributions in the development of this book. You never fell short in helping me where you saw a need when it came to assisting me in bringing this dream to pass.

Lastly, I thank Chanz'e (CMW) for partnering with me and being diligent with providing sound recommendations and revisions to make this book ready for publication. I am truly grateful for your dedication and level of service to the vision of this book.

Introduction

Looking around at the challenges marriages face today, *A Word to the Wife* is timely and impactful. Everywhere you turn, whether you watch the news, read the paper, or talk to people, there is a disconnect going on in the household between husbands and their wives. This disconnect is destroying marriages. On the surface, it might appear as if everything is going well, but the complete opposite is really happening. In marriages worldwide, there is a huge area of opportunity for restoration that is desperately needed.

Despite what circumstances you are currently undergoing, I am glad that you have an open mind to receive what I have written. I am unaware of all the situations you might have been facing that led you to read this book, neither do I know what you came seeking from it, but you will not put this book down and leave the same way that you came to it. While I thank you for reading what has been prepared, I will encourage you that a lot of the matters we face in life are not solved due to our starting something and never quite completing it. So I advise, right from the start, to read the book in its entirety so you view things from a different vantage point, than what you have seen before. In doing so, you will find that the questions that need answers to are actually right in front of you.

I had planned to paint a picture where I wanted you to close your eyes and daydream, but then I realized you wouldn't be able to read with your eyes closed and keep reading. So for purposes of the message that I am trying to convey, I will just ask you to visualize it instead. Envision for a moment, driving and pulling up to a beautiful house on the corner cul-da-sac. You park in front of the two-car garage. Sitting directly in front of you lies a two-story, single-family brick house with white shutters on all the windows.

As you get out of the car, you notice the lush green grass and freshly landscaped lawn with the newspaper strewn in the middle of the yard waiting to be picked up. You head towards the front door and automatically your attention is drawn to the welcome mat of what appears to be a perfect close-knit family. Once on the porch, you notice the door slightly ajar and decide to take a peek on the inside of what appears to be a happy home.

This house is filled to capacity with everything that a man could ever dream of owning on the inside. You bypass all the other rooms and go upstairs to his work and study office with the latest Dell XPS model computer that is positioned in the middle of a mahogany wood desk. Behind the desk, is the chocolate leather desk chair with adjustable wheels, and massage functions, and heat as an added luxury of comfort, which is great for taking quick naps. The large desk has drawers and compartments that are stocked like an office supply store with fountain pens, pencils, notepads, and sticky notes. On the corner of the desk is an 8x10 family portrait

Immediately leaving the office and heading straight down the hallway, is the entertainment room, where the husband and the children enjoy the finest luxuries housed there. On the right side of the room, is a pool table that can easily be converted into both an air hockey and ping pong table. To the left, is the online gaming system with the PS4, XBOX, and the Nintendo Wii. Then there is the Sony HDTV, 3D functionality flat screen mounted on the wall with the high-quality Bose surround sound accompanying it. To top everything off, there is Verizon Fios, and High Speed Internet, and ESPN Sports package with over 400 other channels, where he would never want to leave.

The second to last room upstairs is the exercise room with 400-pound weights, a 40-program trainer voice Treadmill, and Stair Master, and training bike waiting for a workout to begin. The last room is the home library filled with non-fiction, fiction, and all sorts of study materials with no room left on the shelves. Back downstairs, past the kitchen is the backyard. On the back deck is a Weber gas grill ready to be started up. In the middle of the backyard, is a hammock large enough for the husband and family to relax on together. The remaining portions of the house are comprised of everything imaginable that a man could ever desire.

Now that you have the imagery of the house and every room in your mind, imagine the wife and the children going about their daily routines like a family would, but the man is nowhere to be found in the house. Picture searching throughout the entire house, even going out into the yard again, and not finding him where he should be on the gas grill or barbecuing. He is not even lounging in the shade in the hammock relaxing. With all the finest furnishings this house has to offer and with his family he can enjoy it all with, you can't find the man anywhere among it.

As you continue searching for the man of the house, you stoop down to grab the newspaper and your attention is immediately drawn to the man seemingly relaxing up on the "rooftop." He is all alone with nothing to entertain himself. Despite everything on the inside of the house, he seems to be at peace just being there atop the house. Figuratively speaking, I know this image may seem a little bit far-fetched because it's not something that you would probably see. Literally though, I can assure you in many homes all over the world, there are husbands who have emotionally and spiritually retreated to the "rooftop" to find peace and relaxation because down in the house they simply could not find it.

Personally, sometimes the husband may not even be aware that they are on the "rooftop." For several years, I was preparing to write this book for others. I believed God had a message for someone else's home to help the wife bring down their husbands. It wasn't until I allowed my wife Vicky to read the book for the first time, that it was brought to my attention how much I too had moments on the "rooftop." At first, she felt that the book was about us, but I assured her that the book was simply inspired by the scripture in Proverbs and not our home.

The more I heard her words and read the book myself, I had to admit at times, I too had retreated to the "rooftop." Her response made me more sensitive in two aspects. First, that I trust no wife feels that this book at all puts the blame totally on them. This book is a resource tool that will open up what the scripture says about husbands who retreat instead of remain in the house.

I am no subject matter expert, but I am a husband. I am just providing insight from the provision that God gave to me to be a blessing to many marriages. Secondly, it is not my intention to say that a man has the right to even retreat to the "rooftop." To be perfectly honest, not many desire to be on the "rooftop" to begin with. When a husband retreats, it's just an internal response of defense or deflection to escape what in a husband's mind may be an atmosphere uncomfortable for the moment. In the upcoming chapters, you will learn about the attributes, how to assess, how to acknowledge, and how to amend your ways in this process of bringing your husband back in alignment with you.

Chapter 1

Attributes of a Rooftop Husband

Before you as a wife can even begin the quest of identifying the attributes of a "rooftop" husband, which we will certainly address, you have to know that you may not have the slightest inclination that what you are really dealing with is the shell of your husband. I say, shell because what has taken place is the spirit of your husband has retreated to higher ground known as the "rooftop" leaving his shell; outer body to continue trying to operate and satisfy proper husband and fatherly duties. Hopefully, his love for his family and his commitment to God will not allow him to totally abandon or depart the house but that is not always the case. While his body stays and receives all the things the spirit desires to escape, the husband's spirit has gone to the "rooftop" to find peace. The same peace that he was searching for on the inside has led him to pursue it somewhere else, so up he goes to try to obtain what he is missing.

Again, wives may have no idea, and often do not realize

the spirit of her husband is no longer residing there. Let me digress and just state, I will not say 100 percent of the time that the wife is totally clueless about her husband's spiritual whereabouts, but she just misinterprets the signs of him being on the "rooftop" for something else. In keeping with those misinterpretations, there are three attributes that you need to familiarize yourself with. Have you ever felt alone even though your husband is right there with you?

How about the many occurrences where you communicated to your husband that you felt there was no close bond between the two of you? These attributes exist even while you talk and spend—what you believe to be—quality time with each other. It is sad, and you might not want to even admit the facts, but even during times of intimacy, your intuition lets you know that he is just simply not there. This happens more than many care to admit.

Distance

The first attribute you need to be aware of is the one of distance in a "rooftop" husband. He is physically and mentally present in his body, but he has removed his emotions. His spirit has pulled away, leaving his body and mind to go through the motions of what he is required to do just to maintain some form of normalcy. He says and does the things that he is supposed to do, but you know deep down, it just doesn't seem to connect or even add up. For many, the husband may not even say and do the things that are required, which further goes to show his departure to the "rooftop."

The husband has internally distanced himself in an attempt to preserve himself. You might be wondering to yourself; why does he resort to doing this? He doesn't want to leave or knows that he should not leave. This is a coping mechanism for the husband. This prevents him from physically giving up and walking out the door. He distances himself and goes to a place the bible refers to as the "rooftop" (uttermost part of the top of a building).

He is trying to protect himself. You may or may not be cognizant of the facts surrounding what husbands have to battle outside of the home. Were you aware of the verbal and physical strains that come from the attacks at work, in the community, or other places that a husband has to deal with? Outside the home, he has to stand up for himself regularly and fight back. He is faced with challenges that you may never know. The last thing a husband wants is to have to battle the same friction with his wife at home.

Understand, he doesn't want to fight the one he loves. So instead of quarreling with his wife, he pulls away. He does this in hopes that in doing so, that he can avoid conflicts. He separates his emotions so that the words and actions he receives will not add to the damage he has already received coming from outside. I reiterate, it is not his intention to want to physically remove himself, but he distances himself to be able to cope and endure what he considers to be hurt.

Joy by Himself and Others

The second attribute ties right into the first one. Have

you noticed how he seemingly loves to be by himself or with others more than you? It is very hard for wives to understand this attribute. How can a man who has a wife that desires to be with him, loves him, and cares for him desire to be by himself? Better yet, he enjoys someone or something else more than being with his wife. You overhear him laughing and having a great time watching television with his friends while engaged in other activities, but when he is with you, the joy and excitement either does not exist or is not the same as what you observe when he is with others.

During these other activities, the husband is displaying that he can often freely just be himself without fear of judgment. He is in a relaxed frame of mind and can pretty much say or do what his heart desires with a friend. In the event the friend doesn't like what he is saying, they will tell him, get over it, and move on. There is no afterthought of rehashing something he said or did wrong. He doesn't have to worry that it will be held against him somehow. He is in an atmosphere of peace that all husbands love to abide in. When they find this peace, you will see that is where they will be drawn too.

Lack of Passion

The third attribute that goes hand in hand with the last one is the lack of passion. Really, you know, it's not that the husband is not capable of having passion because you see it in him with many other things. You see the drive and hot pursuit he has for other things and people, but for some reason, there is no passion for his wife as it should be or once was. Have you ever asked yourself and wondered where his drive and passion went that at one point he used to have? How could the passion that he had for you somehow vanish and go elsewhere?

You might be puzzled thinking where has his passion and strong affection of love for me and everything else in life gone to. He has left it and gone elsewhere to find it. The "rooftop" husband seems to have lacked the fire and zeal for more in the relationship and settles for just making it through another day. All he is focused on is surviving and being in survival mode. He is just going through the motions of getting by when you know there is no true emotions flowing out of him.

What is it that causes the husband to be distant, desire to be by himself, or with others more than his own wife, and lack passion for what is to bring him joy? The answers to these questions vary for different reasons. However, I have come to give a word to the wife of some of the possible reasons of "why" as you obtain wisdom from Solomon in the Book of Proverbs on the concerns that you face.

Chapter 2

Assess the Situation

The various challenges in marriage mostly cannot be approached with just an analytical process to solve them. One must carefully consider or assess all concerns to gain wisdom on how to correctly address the matter. I am reminded of Paul as he wrote to Timothy, much like I am writing to you, reminding you from 2 Timothy 2:7, *Consider what I say; and the Lord give thee understanding in all things.* In order for anything to have proper resolution, there has to be understanding. The only way to do this is through proper assessment of the situation that is before you.

I am sure that you can recall, times in your marriage, where you faced challenges either now or in the past that were approached irrationally or in an accusatory fashion. Do you remember the outcome? I am sure those reactions didn't do much in the area of resolution, but somehow created more problems. The reason this happens is because there was no accountability in the form of assessing the set of circumstances in the situation first.

Please embark with me and understand that to assess the situation, you have to determine, evaluate, or estimate the value or condition of something. Could it be that is the reason you have not seen the results you have so long sought to see in your marriage? Think on that. This sounds pretty easy to do, but the fact still remains the same, that we are all different and process things entirely different. Ultimately, this makes what should be a simple process quite difficult.

Say you were to ask two or more people to assess the same exact scenario, those same individuals may or may not come up with the same results. The determining factor of how they viewed the scenario is based off how each person views the situation. If we allow everyone to make their assessments based on their own personal emotional or makeup, it's highly probable that various estimations of the situation may occur. However, if a set of guidelines is given for all to use in the form of an assessment; most likely, everyone will come to the same results or at least reach an expected end. For the sole purposes of assessing the situation of the relationship between the husband and wife, our base and guideline principle will be from the Bible.

The Bible contains principles for every single aspect of life as a good baseline and solid foundation that allows us to utilize the same viewpoint as we assess the situation. Isn't it reassuring to know that the Living Word of God is solid and with the proper application, you will see the results? In particular, there are a couple of principles that we should explore as we keep our focus so that we arrive and come to the same result that will be open, honest, and true.

Love

The first principle we need to keep up close and personal in view is that of love. The purpose of *A Word to the Wife* is to strengthen and bring restoration, so there can be a sound relationship in the marriage. If you waver or falter in the arena of love, then this will never happen. What is love? I believe, speaking from personal experience of what I have observed, love is having care and concern about the wellbeing of a person or thing.

Truly, if we say that we love a person, it will be our heart's desire to seek and learn all there is to know about that person, and then do whatever is necessary to support their wellbeing. The Bible tells us in 1 Corinthians 13:4, *Love is patient, love is kind and is not jealous; love does not brag and is not arrogant.* That scripture reference shows us love is longsuffering. This means that love will cause you to endure a lot of things that are not always ideal to reach a certain goal.

It further says, love is kind, is not jealous, does not brag, is not proud, and does not rejoice when wrong happens. Love is happy for truth that is made known, holds up under pressure, believes all things, has hope and never fails. The proof of how we should love is when we realize how much God loves us. God is love and that should be the standard basis of how we treat each other in our marriages.

As you study and mediate on the Word, ask God to reveal to you how this relates to your personal relationship as you reflect on the first principle of love again. It is important to our growth to learn the attributes of love in detail. I am sure there are a lot of books out there that talk on the subject of love, but I recommend you dive deeper into the Bible and learn more by breaking down the text and being a doer of the Word and not just a hearer.

Remember as we start to uncover the state of our situation in our relationship, we must do so in and with love as the priority. If we do not handle what we face with love, the situation will only fester and become worse when we are trying to make the situation better and improve. Let love be the focus. There are three other principles that we will go deeper into as we begin to take a closer look at the situations surrounding us and continue to assess it.

Peace

Now, keeping in line with love, we add to that the second principle of peace. Too often, the home is the greatest battlefield of erupting landmines and a place of war; right alongside the battlefield of the mind, where we deal with our thoughts. In an attempt of trying to make situations better; how many of you know that just trying to discuss a matter of concern sometimes leads or causes a situation to be overanalyzed and completely blown out of proportion? The result is that peace leaves the home. We have all heard the idiom, "making a mountain out of a molehill." That can certainly be avoided if we go about this with peace in mind.

Be sure to understand though that having peace does not mean that there is an absence of conflict or trouble. A lot of times, it is the complete opposite. Having peace means that we remain calm and undisturbed in the midst of struggle and trouble. May I then say, we respond accordingly, operating out of decency and order worthy of being received.

Thinking

The third principle that goes along with the first two and has to be the focus as we go deeper into assessing the situations in our marriage. This is our thought process and the way that we think. I believe, that many don't recognize how powerful the mind and thinking process truly is. If more people understood how our thoughts control the outcome of what we deal with, then they would be more careful when it comes to their thinking.

Here is why. If we are not cognizant or aware of what and how we think, we can create a full scenario that appears real to us, and causes us to believe the wrong things and respond in an incorrect manner in our marriage. Everything starts with a thought. This costly inaccuracy that we thought up, could be the furthest from the truth. But because we were irrational with our thought process, we allowed our minds to think something up and we accepted it as truth.

We are instructed in the scriptures exactly how we are to think. We should only think based off of Philippians 4:8, *Finally, brethren, whatsoever things are true, whatsoever things are honest, whatsoever things are just, whatsoever things are pure, whatsoever things are lovely, whatsoever things are of good report; if there be any virtue, and if there be any praise, think on these things*. Anything that contradicts what is written in the Word as to how we are to think has to be cast down. You just can't accept it. Don't dwell on negative things in your mind as you go to take a closer look at the situation before you.

Refrain from jumping to conclusions at first sight of what you think or feel may be wrongdoing. You need to safeguard your mind from running fast and forming opinions about something that might be secondhand knowledge that you have not witnessed firsthand where you don't know the entire story. Exercise extreme caution when it comes to the challenges that you face in your marriage especially when it comes to your thoughts.

Spoken Words

The fourth is putting into practice of watching the words we speak and how we speak them. We are all familiar with the old saying that children use to say, "sticks and stones may break my bones, but words will never hurt me." It sounded good at the time, but as I grew and became wiser, I learned was not so true. Words create and are extremely powerful so we have to be careful. Many don't even realize that the smallest of words can cause pain within an individual for years after they have been spoken.

The words that we speak should be spoken carefully and with wisdom. The Bible says in Colossians 4:6;

> *Let your speech be always with grace, seasoned with salt, that ye may know how ye ought to answer every man.*

In other words, when we speak of what is wrong or right, we should speak it so that when it is heard, it will bring out flavor to reveal what the matter truly is. The hearer should not be left with a sour reaction to what is heard or turn a deaf ear to what is being communicated.

Another old saying that goes alone with this is, "it is not what we say, but how you say it that matters." I remember clearly the preachers making that a constant reminder. Let us not forget, as we speak of what we find, that we must be mindful to speak the words with the right attitude and motive. What you say could be the truth so clear, but how you say it could prevent it from being received.

After having spent extensive time covering the four main principles of love, peace, thinking, and spoken words, begin the process of assessing the situation of your marriage. This process may not be easy or comfortable, but it must be done. Think of this as a procedure, just as you would when you visit the doctor. The overall assessment of undergoing an examination or an intrusion to sensitive areas is something you desire to avoid because it is in intrusive, but in order to sustain your overall health, it has to be done. However, the good news is, you endure it knowing, after it is all said and done, it will help you to be both healthy and well.

You are one step closer to reaching the ultimate goal of a happier home. No one ever said this was going to be easy because it isn't. To be frank, it is challenging, but if you work through this with an open and honest heart, you will live to see the positive results. I commend your efforts for coming this far by faith by investing to improve your marriage and also helping others with their marriage as well.

Many couples are running on autopilot. Without much thought or action, they each get up every day and go about their normal function as husband and wife. Occasionally, a time of intimacy or passion will happen out of the natural need of the body. Other than this, there is no real driving force that makes them take the time to really love on each other as God intended.

Please by all means, as you take this time to assess the situations, refrain from blaming your husband or either yourself. At this point, it's not a concern of who is as fault, but simply seeing the fault. This is the time you need to step back and look over your marriage. Literally get a paper and pen and make a list of the good, bad, and ugly within your marriage. Go ahead right now and get something to write with so you can start on your list.

Began first with what is good about your marriage. Please don't say there is nothing good about it. I am sure if you think long enough, you will be able to find something; at least, one thing to write down that is good.

Okay. For those that are having a hard time, let me give you the first one and maybe the only one, but it is one. The first good thing about your marriage is that you are married. Don't believe the lie that you would be better by yourself and you don't need your husband.

There are many single people who long to have someone they are married to. There are many lonely people who don't have anyone to work with to start making things better. So even if it seems that you have the raw deal in your husband at least you have someone to work with and that's a good thing. So, I have given you the first good thing for your list, please continue the list of good things.

Now start on the not so good part of your list. Again, refrain from listing blaming actions. Just simply state what you believe is not in place that you desire. For example, instead of saying he never spends time with you or he seems to give more time to other people or things, say there is a lack of intimate fellowship with each other. Or say, I would like to spend more time together. Maybe your list can say there is a need for more support in managing things with the house or children; instead of you don't do anything around the house.

As I stated before, assessing the situation will be a challenge, especially trying to make the list without accusation or blaming. The overall purpose is for you to face the truth that things are not the best and it's time to make steps to improve things. Refuse to continue going through the motions of marriage and began to seek the method that will bring a mutual happiness for your husband and you. It's time that you seek to understand why your husband is there in the house, but his mind and spirit seem to be somewhere else.

Proverbs 1:5 says;

> *A wise man will hear and will increase learning; and a man of understanding shall attain wise counsels.*

In other words, a wise person will take the time to listen and consider something and will grow from what they receive. It also says a person that is able to gain insight into a matter shall acquire or obtain direction.

Assessing the situation of your relationship with your husband is a step of hearing the heartbeat of the marriage. Once you listen and consider the root causes, you will grow in your marriage. Once you get insight into how things are going, you then can get direction on where to go from there. So earnestly, look into the good, bad, and ugly of your marriage. Acknowledge them all and make a conscious decision to go to another level of happiness in your home.

In assessing the situation, the goal is to identify if you have a "rooftop" husband and the causes for him being that way. Although it's tempting to put all the blame on your husband, be open in the next chapter to examining yourself as well to acknowledge your part in the reason your husband is up there.

Chapter 3

Acknowledging Your Part

I want to assure you that *A Word to the Wife* was not at all written to place any sort of blame or accusation totally on the wife as to the reasoning that her husband is on the "rooftop." This book was written as a resource to empower you to thrive and flourish in your marriage. I am simply encouraging you to be steadfast in understanding the full scope of the word that is being both shared and brought forth to you. Provided for you are insights into some of the possible things that you as the wife can do to bring the "rooftop" husband down.

I am sure that you are quite familiar with the famous phrase, "It takes two to tangle." Many wives spend a substantial amount of time trying to fix and change their husbands to be who they want them to be. The truth of the matter is that wives have failed to spend time fixing and working on themselves. That's why *A Word to the Wife* is so important.

It is difficult to take a good hard look at yourself. We have all been there. Have you ever truly stopped and identified those areas that are part of the reason things are not going as well as they could be? It is a must; especially, in the season that we are in, to draw back and take a look in the mirror. Once you do that, acknowledge the role that you have played by taking ownership and holding yourself accountable to any portion of what took place for your husband to arrive on the "rooftop."

In the book of Proverbs, we see several verses of scripture that describe the ways and words of a wife that will cause the husband to retreat to the house top or desire to be in another place within the house. This is clearly shown in the book of Proverbs 21, starting at verse 9.

> *It is better to dwell in a corner of the housetop,*
> *than with a brawling women in a wide house.*

So in order for any kind of acknowledgement to exist, you have to know exactly what is taking place. What actions are contributing to the husband going to the roof?

The word brawling means to cause discord of strife. As I break down the text to ensure that you understand, the verse is simply saying that when a woman constantly causes friction or creates situations between both herself and her husband, it would be better for the husband to pursue trying to find peace in his efforts in just a corner of the housetop, rather than the whole entire house. So a wife should most definitely be mindful on how she goes about handling things so it doesn't cause the husband to have to deal with discord or strife; leaving him no other option but to retreat to the "rooftop."

When a wife tries to initiate bringing to her husband's

attention concerns or issues that may be on her heart, a wife must use extreme caution on how she presents those concerns or pressing issues before her husband's attention, so as not to sow confusion. The wife should be prudent and thoughtful on how to present a light situation that needs to be addressed, so that there will be no actual fighting. You can most definitely start by not pinpointing or starting a sentence with the word, "You."

When that word is used, it puts the husband on the defensive and causes the issue to fester. It is like pointing the finger. The same thing goes with using statements that exaggerate an issue by going back and forth playing the blame game. Don't use language that states, you never and you always. Even if the statement does reflect the truth, there is still another way to best communicate it so you are heard.

In other translations in Proverbs, there are different variations of the word brawling. Take for example in them, they use the world contentious. Instead of brawling, which means argumentative, but the word reflects the same things as we saw before, of having a discord or strife. In Proverbs 21:19 says;

> *It is better to dwell in the wilderness, than with a contentious and an angry woman.*

A wife that often wants to spend time debating, arguing, or trying to prove she is right and her husband is wrong, will cause the man to retreat or draw back from the house completely. As I made reference in this book earlier, men have to compete with those in the office or outside the house, and they don't want to have to come home and be in opposition or a battle with their wife.

Proverbs 27 Verse 15 compares a contentious woman to a continual dropping in a very rainy day. A continuing dripping slowing causes damage to that which it is dripping onto and causes a ripple effect. A wife who is full of contention also breaks the calm and silence in the house, causes damage in the relationship with their husband, and it will sooner or later effect other areas of the couple's life. Just like a continual dripping, a contentious woman can be irritating. These ways of a wife will cause a man to be a "rooftop" husband.

The words that a wife uses needs to be examined because the types of words that she speaks to her husband can be helpful, harmful, or detrimental. Alongside, the types of words that are used, is the tone of the words that are spoken. In Proverbs 12:18, it says,

> *There is that speaketh like the piercings of a sword: but the tongue of the wise is health.*

I believe, because husbands in their wives eyes are strong and tough, that they fail to understand that their words can cut and pierce to the very marrow of the heart and spirit of even the strongest man. Reflect on that. That should not happen, but we all fall short. But if this is done too often without a place of rest in the home, this will cause the husband to seek an atmosphere of peace elsewhere.

Just as I mentioned above, the wife must be prudent

and selective with the words that she uses to relay the message and information to her husband. In Proverbs 15:1 says, *A soft answer turneth away wrath: but grievous words stir up anger.* As the wife, you need to be mindful of your words and how you speak them, lest what you speak be a hurt, than words that heal. I remind you that the Bible tells us just how powerful the tongue is.

I believe, the brawling, contentious attitude and words that are harsh from the wife all has a root cause. The root cause sometimes is because of things the husband has done, said, or neglected to do or say. That is in no way excusable at all, but there has to be a common ground between a husband and his wife. Then again, at other times, it's because of things others have done in the past to the wife. She is now allowing the past pain to be brought into the current relationship with the husband. That is why in Proverbs 21:19 says,

> *It is better to dwell in the wilderness, than with a contentious and an angry woman.*

Most often, the pain that stems from the afflictions that the wife received from not being treated right by her husband, or the pain from past hurts from former lovers, or male family members comes out of anger towards her husband. It is like a "crying out" for help. She sees and remembers the pain of the past and refuses to allow it to be repeated. Her emotions are her lashing out to protect herself. She loves her husband, but is really trying to say, I don't want to be hurt again. The energy is channeled in the wrong way and it comes out as rage.

Proverbs 30:21-23 names four things that causes the earth to be disquieted and that it cannot bear. Disquieted means to be troubled or tremble. One of these is an odious or hateful woman when she is married. Remember, a wife that has hatred in her life because of what the husband may or may not have done or said, and for her past relationships, will drive her husband to the "rooftop" to avoid having to deal with the outburst of anger and hatred. Reflect back over your marriage and just be willing to acknowledge if you have been a wife who is brawling, contentious, sharp with your words, or responding in anger and hatred from current or past pain.

If by chance you do acknowledge or recognize any of these areas of opportunity, then move to Chapter 4 to amend your ways. If for some reason, you don't believe that you fall into any of these reason that could cause your husband to be a "rooftop husband," then praise God for that. Begin to pray and ask God to reveal to you any areas that need to be made known so that you can be able to acknowledge any part that you have in the marriage being in the shape that it is in. This will help you to amend your ways as you will learn in the next chapter.

Chapter 4

Amend Your Ways

I believe that the next three principles that I reveal to you, when practiced, will draw your husband down from the "rooftop." They have to be applied first. You first became aware of the attributes of a "rooftop" husband. After that, you then assessed the situation. Acting upon the assessment, you then acknowledged your part or role in why your husband has transcended to the "rooftop." Now, the only thing left to do is to bring everything together and amend.

Despite the things that you might have acknowledged in the previous chapters, or what other things might have been made known to you, try to proceed and practice what I am sharing here with you, instead of what you acknowledged was in error. This will establish the things that are needed to lead your relationship to where it ultimately needs to be to thrive. This is as good a time as any to begin to amend.

Release Control

Each principle has two words. The first word in each

principle begins with the letter "r" and the second word begins with the letter "c." The first principle that might seem challenging at first, but that you must learn, is the art of how to "release control." I felt the resistance from some. I must restate it again. You must learn to "release control." You might be asking yourself deep down; release control of what?

Release the control of trying in your own might to fix your husband and your marriage. Sometimes the wife tries to play Mrs. Fix It because she somehow believes that she understands the root cause of what the problem is. That just might very well be the case. However, she has to come to the realization that most attempts to trying to fix what is wrong, is often misunderstood as the wife trying to control her husband or question his authority to lead. Most men will fight this to the death. Be sure to keep as a focal point that only God can change the heart and mind of your husband, so release the idea that you can fix him or show him how to make things better.

Before going deeper into this principle, I want to give you a minute to recover from the first release of relinquishing control. This is going to take diligence and practice because it is not an easy thing to do. Once you start applying this to your daily life, it will be that much easier for you to release the control of the house also. God has a set designed order. Please note, within every man, is the natural desire to lead and be in control. Many husbands who feel like they don't have control will automatically retreat before they fight their wives for control.

Might that be the reason you see him engaged with his friends and he is having a good time, and you wonder why his mood changes when he is away from you. With all of the good intention that you may have by making that phone call to get someone to come in and fix that leak or broken pipe, it sends the wrong signal to your husband. What it says is that you don't need him. Your motives might be right to you but will come off wrong if you do this. Let your husband do what God created him to do.

Now, I know that you might be thinking to yourself that if you don't make that call, it won't get done. I pray that you come to be enlightened that statement may not always be true. A good husband will not sit back and allow his house to go down or be in disarray. It might not get done like you want it, and when you want it, but if you step back and give your husband the chance to take the control. Allow God to move on his heart to do what needs to be done because you have been praying for that.

Once you release the controls to your husband in the house, it's okay to give signals and alerts to what needs attention in the house in a loving and none nagging way. It would be good to highlight nagging way as an emphasis here. Have you ever taken notice of the latest car models that have the front and back sensors that make a beeping noise and let the driver know they are approaching an object? These sensors just give the signal, but it's up to the driver to adhere to the signal and take control and stop or turn the wheel on its own. That is what this is an example of.

I know for me, there would be several parking spaces that I would have passed up and missed out on. However, I was about to receive the alert and proceed with caution sometimes and still get to park. Then at other times, I gave heed to the signal and went to find another spot. Again, because the driver has the control, they can be on the alert of what the signal is saying, but because they are in control, they can still make the judgement call whether to continue or change.

Reverence Command

Moving right along to the next principle is to "reverence commands" of your husband. To reverence is to give honor or deep respect. In this instance, the wife needs to begin to practice respect and honor the husband's commands. Let's be perfectly honest. The word command is a very strong word and carries with it negative connotations and it can be a demeaning tone as well for some. Oftentimes, people take offense if they feel they are being commanded to do something.

The word command does not have to be taken negatively, nor does it have to be taken as if you are lower than the one giving it. To command, simply means, to request, instruct, or direct something or someone in the way it should be done or go. Let's lighten the mood a little because I know this is a lot of information to absorb. Consider a command as a polite request. You can laugh here.

Referring back to God's order for the home, the man is the head. A wife should reverence directions or requests that her husband provides for the home. In so doing, she is not only honoring her husband, but God as well. Before you begin thinking of how to reverence your husband's commands, let's look at things we should not do first that will not give reverence. It is unwise to make your husband feel that his ideas and instructions are inferior to yours, or that they don't carry weight or have merit. Don't undermine or belittle his commands; especially, in front of your children or others. The same thing goes for trying to override or change his commands because you think your ideas were or are better.

In these days and times, many wives have just as much knowledge, and sometimes even more than her husband. This is where the heart of submission comes into play. The wife should give her thoughts and signals to her husband and then trust God and him to lead the house in the way that God directs and instructs the man to go. To show reverence to his commands, means to listen intently as he speaks. Don't interrupt him when he is talking but allow him to get his full thoughts out before you question it. Don't be so quick to challenge him or try to alter the communication without getting an understanding of why he has directed it the way he did.

Let's go further. Of course, there are times when even the best leaders make the wrong decisions and give commands that fail or were not the best. Even in the midst of this, the wife should be careful to reverence those choices and not fall into the trap of saying, I told you so or insinuating they should have done it your way. On the contrary, she should lovingly undergird her husband and support him in the next move for the house to correct things or choose another course of action.

Respect Choices

This final principle may seem similar or closely related

to "reverence commands," but there is a difference. The principle is for the wife to "respect choices" of her husband. The command of reverence deals with the direction of the house. When it comes to respecting the choices of your husband, these are things that are personal to him. It could be something as simple as respecting what he likes, where the wife can either join in with him, or allow her husband to enjoy them on his own.

Now, I am not speaking of respecting choices that are damaging to the wife, husband, children, or the house. Respect the fact that if he chooses to walk around the house barefoot, than wear slippers. You know, respect his wishes to not have to wear a tie when it's not required. Grab him a brand new tie from time to time. It was meant to make you smile. You might think that these may seem silly or simple; maybe, they actually are, but I pray that you are receptive to the principle that I am trying to get across.

I am naming these simple choices as a place to start. They can get even more complex than what I have shared, but at least you have a basis in which to follow. Regardless of how simple or complex, as a wife, respect the man of the house and his choices. You and your husband are two different individuals with completely different tastes, ideas, and viewpoints trying to mesh two worlds together to become one. You may have a lot of things in common, but everything does not have to be common.

So if he enjoys watching certain types of television sports shows or movies that are decent and in order; even though they might not be what you prefer, respect his preferences. It is quite beneficial to sit down and learn to watch them, even if you don't like it, just to spend time with him. Be willing to compromise. Also, know that there will be times where your husband will want to have time alone or to hang out with friends every now and again. There is nothing wrong with that. There has to be balance.

Again, two different people with similarities and differences that are bringing everything together operating on one accord. Once you start building on the bond, you will find more things that each of you like to do, that the other one doesn't. This is normal. You were created to be a help meet. There just has to be respect for a marriage to work. To bring the principles to a close; keep in mind, that as long as the choices don't harm others, him or you, respect your husband and stand with him. He will be sure to do the same for you by respecting you.

So as we recap, in order to amend your ways practice the principles. You will start to notice that the atmosphere of your home will shift; making it a place your husband will run to and not retreat from. Relinquish your need to be in control and stop trying to get your husband to be somebody else. There is no need for you to run the house. Reference the commands that your husband provides in trying to guide and lead you and the home. To sum it all up, simply respect choices that are not damaging to your home, him, or you.

By proper application of what has been provided to you, you will walk in these principles and create an atmosphere that will draw your husband back into the house with all of his being. He will be in a place where he feels comfortable and be the man that God created him to be. He will be in comfort and not feel threatened or feel that he has to be in opposition to his wife. It will be a place that he runs to with joy and gladness, and not withdraw from to protect his mind and spirit. Love your husbands with the love of Christ and continue to keep him lifted in prayer. Let God work on your husband so the marriage can be the covenant that God originally designed.

Chapter 5

Final Words

In *A Word to the Wife* subtitle, you will notice the book has the word "bring" in it. In order to bring something, you have to be in tune with it. Basically, you have to have a connection to it. Could it be that what you are uncovering here is that you were out of balance because there was no connection being made? Knowing that you are trying to bring your husband down from the "rooftop," you have to be willing to go where he is and make a connection.

Remain Connected

So in addition to the commands previously mentioned in Chapter 4 Amend your Ways, the fourth and final command that you will also want to apply and put into practice is to "remain connected." Remember that a wife should remain connected even when the husband goes to the "rooftop," lest she become distant, find joy in others, and loose her lack of passion. Now, I am not at all saying that you have to get into the frame of mind he is in and be like him. I am not saying that at all.

You need to comprehend what he is doing and what it is that causes him to withdraw from you. You have to do what it takes to bring him down and reel him back in to you. It is going to take time. You are going to have to be persistent with your efforts. You must exercise patience because the retreating that draws a husband to the "rooftop" is done over time.

You have to be careful about how you attempt to bring him down from the "rooftop" because if you connect in the wrong way as you bring him down, he may retreat back. Even after you have brought your husband down, don't fall into the former things that led him there in the first place. The whole idea is to keep him from headed back to where he just left. In all actuality, bringing your husband down, may not be just a one-time assignment. Because you are both human beings, it is likely that either of you will fall into the same pattern that will cause you to have to apply what you have learned for many years to come. A marriage has to be worked at.

In closing, I want to share this last thought with you. I don't believe there is a such thing as a bad marriage because God says in Proverbs 18:22;

> *Whoso findeth a wife findeth a good thing, and obtaineth favour of the Lord.*

He also said that marriage is honorable in all and the bed is undefiled (Hebrews 13:4). It is not the marriage that is bad, but the people who fail to practice the principles that will keep the fire burning in the relationship.

So you have come all this way and might feel that this book only focused on the things the wife needs to do, stop, or change, and you are correct. This book was intentionally created and geared towards the wife; to share a word that will encourage them to draw their husbands back in an intimate covenant relationship with them. I pray continued blessings upon you that God will speak to you in ways that He has never spoken to you before.

Before I sign off here, let me share with you that I am beginning the vision for the next book in the series entitled, *A Word to the Husband: How to Love Your Wife as Christ Loved the Church.* I will direct and focus my attention on the husbands next as I share a word that will help them walk in Christ ordained love for you. So as you wait on *A Word to the Husband*, begin to walk in what was revealed in *A Word to the Wife*. Remember two shall become one. That is what this is all about.

It is time to rekindle the flame and enjoy what God has done in your life. I wrote a poem back in 2005 that I thought might kick start the flame burning for you that was inspired by God. You are married because a fire was once in your heart towards your mate. I hope that *A Word to the Wife* was the spark that you needed to get the fire back in your marriage.

Keep the Fire Burning

By Bernard Blackmon

"Love is like a flame that needs fuel to keep it burning.
To keep love ablaze in your marriage,
there are things you need to keep churning.

Trust, honor, and respect should be active each and every day.
Encouragement, affection, and kind words will keep the
passion of love where it needs to stay.

Be sure to guard from all elements that will eventually
put the fire out. From the greatest strain of unfaithfulness;
to the smallest seeds of jealous and doubt.

Love just like a flame if neglected will soon fade away.
So give attention to keep the fire burning;
for getting it started again, could be a high price to pay."

— Bernard Blackmon, inspired by God, 2005

About the Author

Pastor Bernard Blackmon was born on August 17, 1968, in Washington, D.C. He attended the Washington, D.C. public school system, graduating from H.D. Woodson Sr. High on June 4, 1986. In January 1987 he entered into the Marine Reserves. His term with the Marines Reserves lasted for eight years. During his military time he traveled many places and was summons to active duty to participate in the Gulf War in Saudi Arabia.

Pastor Blackmon was brought up from a child at Faith Temple No. 2 OFWB church, where he served faithfully until his called to launch Kingdom Seekers Fellowship Church. Bishop L. N. Forbes is the founding pastor of Faith Temple No. 2 and Bishop LaVaughn Hughes is currently serving as pastor.

Pastor Blackmon accepted Christ into his life on January 14, 1990 and acknowledged the presence of the Holy Spirit in his life in November 1990. He has attended several Bible Classes taught at Faith Temple No. 2 and has taken Bible Courses over the internet, but his greatest joy is his private study and prayer time, where he sets himself to Hear from God.

Pastor Blackmon began preaching on March 7, 1993. His first sermon was "A Hunger And Thirst for the Right Thing," coming from Matthew 5:6. He was ordained an Elder of the Middle Eastern District of the OFWB Conference in November 1994. His greatest memories of preaching the gospel came from his missionary trips to Haiti in 1997 and Liberia in 2012. He has taught Teenage Bible Class, and was a Sunday School Teacher for many years. He has been a Choir Director and a Praise & Worship Leader. He has written and directed several plays. He was the President of the Young People Christian League Convention (YPCL) in the Middle Eastern District of the OFWB Conference for 17 years.

Pastor Blackmon was a volunteer leader in the Young Life youth ministry in Southern Princes Georges County, MD for over six years. He also helped teach Bible Study in the Lorton, VA, Youth Facility for over four years.

He was married to his wife Vicky, on September 7, 1996. They have two miracle children Asia Monet (1997) and Bre'nard Aquor (1998).

He released a gospel CD of songs he wrote entitled, "You Shall Be Saved" in October 2005. These songs can be found on several digital download sites on the Internet.

Pastor Blackmon started in the Federal Government in March 1988. He has been with the Department of Treasury since October 1998, where he served as the Local President of the Christian Employee Organization, (Christian Fundamentalist

Internal Revenue Employees) CFIRE for 4 years and was the Northeast Regional VP of the National CFIRE Board for 4years.

Pastor Blackmon has a great love for God and His people. His favorite scripture and life testimony is Matthews 6:33;

> *Seek ye, first the kingdom of God and His righteousness and all these things shall be added unto you.*

Pastor Blackmon planted the Kingdom Seekers Fellowship Church on February 28, 2014 where he preached the opening message "Seize The Kingdom." Kingdom Seekers Fellowship Church is a growing church and they are striving to live out its foundation scripture Matthews Chapter 6 verses 33 and church motto: "Converted To Christ, Committed To Church and Caring For The Community."

Pastor Blackmon has now multiplied to his tenure by obtaining authorship with his first literary work entitled, *A Word to the Wife*. His passion and vision for this series was birthed from revelation pertaining to his biblical studies from the Book of Proverbs. The wisdom imparted will change the capacity in which marriages were functioning and allow them to operate as God originally intended. He is currently working on the next book in the series entitled, *A Word to the Husband: How to Love Your Wife as Christ Loved the Church*.

Need additional copies?

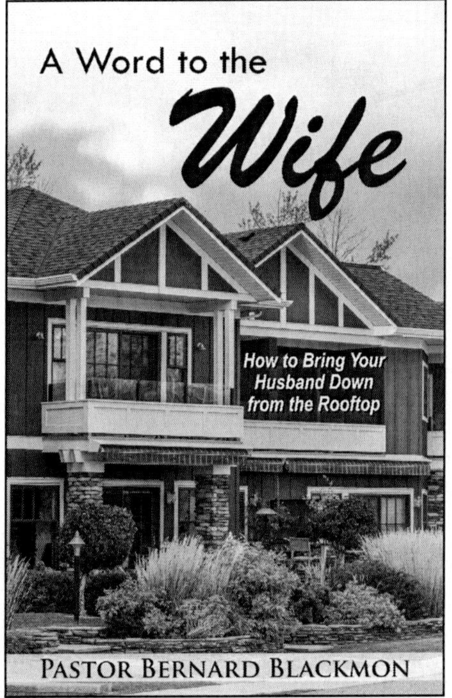

To order more copies of

A Word to the *Wife*

contact CertaPublishing.com

- Order online at: CertaPublishing.com/AWordToTheWife
- Call 855-77-CERTA or
- Email Info@CertaPublishing.com